Fusion Kitsch
POEMS FROM THE CHINESE OF

HSIA YÜ

TRANSLATED

BY

STEVE BRADBURY

ZEPHYR PRESS

BROOKLINE, MASSACHUSETTS

Publication was assisted by a grant from the Massachusetts Cultural
Council and the Tiny Tiger Foundation.

Cover painting by Hsia Yü
Cover and book design by *typeslowly*
Text set in Minion and MingLiu
Printed in Michigan by McNaughton & Gunn

Library of Congress Control Number: 2001 131791

98765432 FIRST PRINTING
ZEPHYR PRESS
50 KENWOOD STREET   BROOKLINE, MA 02446
www.zephyrpress.org

MASSACHUSETTS CULTURAL COUNCIL

Grateful acknowledgment is made to the following publications in which versions of many of the translations in *Fusion Kitsch* first appeared: *Chain*, *Chung-Wai Literary Monthly*, *Fine Madness*, *Frontier Taiwan*, *Inter-Asia Cultural Studies*, *Jacket*, *Literary Imagination*, *Poetry International*, *Tinfish*, *tofu*, and *Two Lines*.

腹語術

早期及未結集之詩

FUSION KITSCH

TRANSLATOR'S PREFACE

Hsia Yü (or Xia Yu, as her name is sometimes spelled) was born in Taiwan but now divides her time between Paris and Taipei, where she makes a living as a lyricist and translator and enjoys a much-deserved reputation for being one of the most interesting and provocative poets writing in Chinese today. The author of four volumes of poetry, she first came to attention in the mid-1980s with the appearance of *Memoranda* (*Beiwanglu*), a self-published collection of poems and poetic memoranda whose brassy and iconoclastic tone struck a deeply sympathetic cord in Taiwan's younger readers as they stood poised on the expectant edge of the country's entry into our alleged culture of global capital. More important perhaps for her subsequent critical reputation, Hsia Yü's frank and innovative treatment of gender and sexuality in a small handful of poems in this collection and in her second collection *Ventriloquy* (*Fuyushu*) was seized upon by critics and scholars anxious to find a candidate to fill the long-vacant post of "Chinese feminist poet."

But while Hsia Yü may well have been one of the first woman poets writing in Chinese to have written about love and romance in a manner that broke dramatically from the conventions and constraints of traditional Chinese women's poetry, if we bother to look beyond labels at the poetry itself, we will find a body of work that is far less interested in providing a critique of gender relations or advancing a sexual/textual agenda than in exploring the sensuous and quirky interface between the pleasures of the flesh and the pleasures of the text. It is this preoccupation with pleasure that sets Hsia Yü apart from other poets writing in Chinese today; that and the fact that her poetry embodies a *fusion* of styles and influences—both high and kitsch—with the French influence running perhaps stronger than most. This is not to say—I hasten to add—that French letters or culture have exerted any direct influence on Hsia Yü's poetry; it is simply that, like many a French poet, she has a particular fascination with the "music" and materiality of language, which, in Hsia Yü's case, is not the French language, of course, but the Chinese language. Indeed, much of the pleasure of reading her poetry derives from the ambience and evocative "airs" that seem to arise out of the very sound and shape of her words and phrasing.

And so we come to my own contribution to *Fusion Kitsch*. Of the 40 poems I have translated for this volume, the lion's share are from Hsia Yü's most recent and most powerful collection, *Salsa* (1999), which gathers her poems from the closing decade of our late *fin de millénium*. The remaining translations are from her other collections; the two I mentioned earlier and a third (and rather singular) collection I did not, titled *Rub: Ineffable* (*Moca: Wuyimingzhuang*). This last is less a collection of individual poems than a montage of evocative fragments and found poems the poet culled from the cut-and-paste "ruins" of her previous collections and published in 1996 in an elegant folio edition with the pages left untrimmed in the grand manner of the *belle époque*. In the interest of showcasing her more recent work, I have taken the liberty of arranging this sampling of her poetry in the reverse order in which her collections appeared in print.

I have also taken the liberty of taking certain liberties with the text, as translators are wont to say. A liberal approach seemed inevitable to me, or so I would like to think, and most of my departures have amounted to little more than the addition of a word or two to draw out the meaning or implications of a word or phrase. Others were of a more substantial nature, such as the addition of a rhythmic feature or foreign word or phrase where my English seemed insufficiently resonant to evoke the ambience or force of the original. As *Fusion Kitsch* is a parallel-text edition of the poems of Hsia Yü, bilingual readers can, of course, consult the original poems, while readers without Chinese are free to turn to the Translator's Notes at the end of this volume, where they will find my significant departures dutifully logged. Not that I have ever departed very far from the original—the text was always there to draw me back again; as was Hsia Yü, although less, as one might think, to control my representation of her work than to preserve its openness. Readers need their freedom, she has often insisted, even that most aggressive of reader, the translator.

I have been very fortunate that Hsia Yü has worked closely with me on these translations. Her contribution to *Fusion Kitsch* has been invaluable. For her generosity in sharing her manuscripts and for her patience in glossing her work and reading and commenting on the many drafts of my translations I sent her way, I owe the poet a great debt of thanks. I would also like to thank her for allowing Zephyr Press to use one of her paintings for the cover art. Finally, I would like to thank the many friends and associates who have read and commented on drafts of my translations or helped in other significant ways to see *Fusion Kitsch* to completion: John Balcom, David Barton, Naifei "Fifi" Ding, Howard Goldblatt, M.A. Greenstein, Stuart Hopen, Hung Hung, Jerome Li (first and foremost), Wenchi Lin, Sylvia Marijnissen, Amie Parry, and (last but far from least) my editor at Zephyr Press, Christopher Mattison.

FROM *SALSA* (1999)

你正百無聊賴我正美麗

只有咒語可以解除咒語
只有祕密可以交換祕密
只有謎可以到達另一個謎
但是我忽略健康的重要性
以及等待使健康受損
以及愛使生活和諧
除了建議一起生一個小孩
沒有其他更壞的主意
你正百無聊賴
我正美麗

You are so very very bored I am so very beautiful

Only a spell can remove a spell
Only a secret trade on secrets
Only a mystery arrive at another mystery
But I neglect the importance of health
And waiting leaves health subject to abuse
And loving makes for a harmonious life
Apart from suggesting we have a child together
I have no worse idea than this
You are so very very bored
I am so very beautiful

最熟最爛的夏天

夏天沉落在貓眼的鐘面
沉落在栗子色的四肢

17塊一籃的桃子
第4天就開始爛的夏天

曠日廢時地吃著飯整個春天
專注於光顏色和氣氛

觀察葡萄藤的影子移動
後期印象派的最後一個傍晚

光點在吊床上加深
在風吹起的簾子上變淺

顯著的筆觸分割
加上最後一點葡萄就裂開了

這時候已經是8月
差不多要進入野獸派

再也不能滿足於光
同時對氣氛厭倦

最熟最爛的夏天
厄言如葡萄蔓衍

The Ripest Rankest Juiciest Summer Ever

Summer sinks into the clock-face of the cat's eye
Sinks into chestnut colored limbs

A 17 franc basket of peaches
Day four and already summer has run from ripe to rank

All spring long we dined as if we had all the time in the world
Followed with interest the color, light and atmosphere

Observed the shadows of the grapevines advancing to this
Last evening of the postimpressionists

The dabs of light thicken on the hammock
Grow thin on the windblown curtain

Each stroke acquiring definition
Until the last stroke added bursts grape-skin

Must be August
Ripe for the Fauvists

Never again will mere light so delight us
And O how we weary of atmosphere

Our idle conversation spreads like vines in the arbor
In this ripest rankest juiciest summer ever

同時對風格厭倦
風格到底存不存在

風格像雪
雪是多麼多麼容易弄髒啊

雖然雪並不存在
吊床更存在

比四月的鳶尾花，6點鐘的茴香酒
絕不比一場現場轉播足球賽

來訪的客人研究中國古代建築
他說現今唯武裝革命最富悲劇性

另外就是足球賽
我們這樣曠日廢時地吃著飯

煙燻鮭魚，螃蟹和龍蝦
有人說你看這樣肥大的生蠔

如何讓我們的左派傾向
找到出口呢

1906 年，路上遇雨的塞尚回到工作室
脫下外套和呢帽，面窗躺著

注意到桌上傾倒一籃蘋果　The appleness
of the apples　蘋果和它的倒影，三個骷髏頭，

And O how we weary of style
Does style, after all, exist

So like the snow
Defiled at the merest touch

But even though the snow does not exist
The hammock is more manifest than ever

More than an April iris or an aperitif at six
Although compared to soccer broadcast live hardly anything exists

Our guest, an enthusiast of "Old Cathay," asserts that in these fallen days
Only armed revolution presents so many tragic implications

And then there is soccer
O how we dine as if we had all the time in the world

Smoked salmon, crab and lobster
And will you look at the size of this oyster

If we could but find the proper outlet and the sympathies
To release our leftist tendencies

1906, Cézanne, caught in a storm, returns to his studio
Removes his hat and coat and collapses by the window

Taking stock of the table, its overturned basket of apples, he notices
The "appleness of the apples" and their shadows, the three skulls

衣櫃和水壺，陶罐
半開的抽屜，時鐘

他想到比例並不那麼重要
桌線對不對齊並不那麼重要

他死了
閉緊的眼皮上對直的那條線是三點鐘的鐘面。

這樣是不夠的
下面輪到馬蒂斯

The wardrobe, the pitcher, the crock
The half-opened drawer, the clock

It occurs to him proportion is hardly worth making a fuss about
He will not fret over whether the table is level or not

He closes his eyes and dies
His eyelids trace a line pointing straight to three o'clock

Still, there is something wanting in all this
Must be time for Matisse

你不覺得她很適合早上嗎？

為 Yan 寫給一個塞內加爾女人

你不覺得她
她很適合早上嗎？
你不覺得她很適合
譬如說
奔跑

她適合打開她的舊餅乾盒
讀潮溼的舊信
她像一個軟木塞
封著一瓶酒　　你不覺得她很適合匆忙奔跑
過一個燦爛的星空嗎
她適合意志
她也適合　　再舉一個例子說
她適合優美地滑倒

你不覺得她是可以擦掉的嗎
那種一修再修的草圖
但她的拇指浮現

你不認為她
她就是很適合摩擦嗎？
你不認為
她適合早上來到？

16

Don't you feel the morning becomes her?

For Yan for a Senegalese woman

Don't you feel
The morning becomes her?
Don't you feel that it becomes her?
Running
For instance

Opening an old cookie tin becomes her
Reading all the old damp letters
She is the very image of a cork
In a wine bottle. Don't you feel that
Bolting 'cross a starry sky becomes her?
Having a will of her own becomes her
And other things become her too. For instance
A graceful fall becomes her

Don't you feel that you could rub her right away
She is just that kind of ink
But then you find her thumbprint reappearing right before your eyes

Don't you feel that
Rubbing becomes her?
Don't you feel that
Coming in the morning becomes her?

夢見波依斯

看完你的展覽回來就夢見你
你不喜歡你四方形的墳
你說你要一種多角形的
我接著夢見你用毛氈包裹的
那架三角鋼琴。我夢過多次死亡
沒有一次這麼接近一架鋼琴
我寫過很多次鋼琴
也從來沒有像過一頭象

不斷重複的紀錄片裡
你在你的屋子裏走來走去帶一頂氈帽
穿著你的藍布褲和釣魚背心
看起來你什麼也沒做只是走來走去
走得很慢——概念式地走——走如何
是概念式的？走的方式。其循環
其封閉性。1959 年，你構想中的一個作品
是想像一個「進不去的工作間」

但看起來你什麼也沒做
把一個梯子搬到另一個地方
爬上去——爬得很慢——站在上面一下下
又爬下來　把一個什麼東西用毛氈
包起來　把一塊冷凍油脂放在膝背
壓扁　突然逼近鏡頭

「相遇的方式很重要」你說

Dreaming Beuys

For Joseph Beuys (1921-1986)

Home from your show at the Pompidou I dream of you
You are not very happy with your grave
You say you want a polyhedron not the customary four-sided hole
Then I dream of that grand piano you wrapped in felt
I've often dreamt of death but no death I ever dreamt of took me half
This close to a piano and I've often written of pianos but no piano
I ever wrote of ever looked half this much like an elephant

In the film loop I see you in a room
Walking back and forth in your fishing vest
Your blue jeans and ubiquitous felt hat
It doesn't look as if you're doing very much but walking back
And forth, slowly, conceptually — How does one in fact walk
Conceptually? — A manner of walking. Cyclically.
Hermetically. One of the works you dreamt up in '59
The Trans-Siberian Railway conceived as an "unenterable workroom"

But I can't really say I see much work going on here
You move the ladder across the room then climb to the top —
You climb very slowly — stand for a bit then climb back down
Wrap something up in your signature felt and press
A piece of frozen lard behind your knee and slowly squeeze it flat
When you are suddenly confronting the camera

"The manner of the meeting was important" you say

那是一個幸福極了的年代
大家被偶發的概念迷惑
被厭煩蠱動——
厭煩初始，帶著光
溫暖　神聖　溼潤
你只需要用一塊毛巾
遮住了額頭以下的臉
那頭象就從來沒有這麼像過你
比起那架鋼琴

遲來的我參觀你的作品
走過那些安靜的物
被迫參加你的裝置變成你的材料
這個午後乃是稀有當我
站在一面大窗漏進的光裏與
所有你的物品相遇

我承認我的確被迷惑。這些石塊木板
蠟燭瓶子錫罐電線電池雪橇
乾草麻繩。變壓器。電話機。
布偶。腳架。水桶。提琴。
我凝視一個衣架一個紙箱
紙箱裡一塊油脂油脂上插著
溫度計　　它們可是
你那簡潔　疏離而又戲謔的
靈魂轉世——但儘可能地
予以改裝和倒置　以緄帶和熨斗的方式
出現

What a phenomenally fortunate age yours was
So many held spellbound by the concept of "the happening"
So many bitten by the bewitching worm of boredom and ennui —
In the beginning of boredom and ennui
There was light and warmth and moisture and a touch of the divine
You appear with a cloth simply draped across your lofty brow
And that elephant has never been more like you
Much less your thick-skinned Beckstein grand

I missed your age but I arrive at your retrospective
And stroll by these tranquil objects until I find
Myself a willy-nilly conscript of your ensemble
On this rare afternoon standing bathed in the light
Pouring through the glassy curtain walls
Encountering all these objects you have made your own

I have to admit I find myself quite spellbound by these objects: wood,
Stone, bottles, candles, wire, batteries, and aluminum cans. The snow-
Sled and the twine. The clumps of straw. The transformer. The
Telephone. The cloth doll. The tripod. The bucket. The violin.
My eyes fall upon the coat-rack and the card-board box
And in the box the wedge of lard and in the lard
The thermometer thrust in the middle. Might these objects not be
The scattered afterlife of your pithy and impious soul —
But now entirely refurbished and turned on its ear by your
Intervention of adhesive-bandage and the iron

Just so have I walked by this piano you have wrapped in felt
The same one I will later dream of — but Beuys
If it's just a question in the end of who wraps who
I think I have the upper hand here for I can wrap you in a dream.

就這樣我走過那架被包起來的鋼琴
它就像我即將夢見的樣子——你知道
波依斯，如果最後無非就是
誰把誰包起來的問題　　我想
我佔了優勢。我用夢包裹你。
然後用詩包裹夢。因
你先我而死。我把燈關掉。把你的
傳記闔起來。把印有你照片的
明信片寄掉。把為你寫的詩印出來
什麼人即要讀到。我隔著讀
讀他的讀——

但是關於厭煩
唉我的厭煩依然
比不上你的厭煩
因你到達之厭煩乃厭煩之
太初與極致——
想及此而無限加倍的厭煩

恐怕就超過了你的
但我的厭煩很快又要被
後面那個更令人厭煩的傢伙超越
最後你知道嗎波依斯
就變成誰比誰煩的問題

And wrap that in a poem. And simply because
You have signed out before me. And I turn out the light. And I close
Up your bio. And I mail off the postcard with your picture
On it. And I print out the poem I have made for you someone
Somewhere will one day read. And then somewhere
Somehow I will one day read their reading . . .

And so we return to boredom and ennui
I doubt if I could be half as fed up as you were
For you made it state-of-the-art
World without end
But I have no sooner thought this thought than
I find myself more fed up than ever

I'm afraid my boredom and ennui will soon be overtaking your own
But then it won't be long before mine is overtaken by
The boredom and ennui of the nudnik coming up behind us
Beuys so in the end I guess it all comes down to a problem of
Each one more fed up than the last

繼續討論厭煩

所以我們必須繼續討論厭煩
厭煩的東西都是厭煩的
任何厭煩的東西都是厭煩的
事實上只有厭煩的東西才是
厭煩的
它不必被發現，它在。

它有一種遙遠而清澈的感覺
有一點瘋狂
也有懷舊和戰慄的情愫
其實也離道德不遠

你要怎麼形容厭煩的味道呢？
只有最老成持重的侍者會說：
「你要怎麼形容橘子的味道呢
我們只能說有些味道像橘子。」

讓人著迷的不是它的建築
而是它的癱瘓。有一種瀧涎香。
琥珀色。也不妨甚至
像是一些呆滯的水管的樣子。
一些牛皮紙袋的樣子。
機緣、回憶、慾望和巧合
的反向下水道的歷史向度之下的城市

那真是一種氣氛的問題
厭煩
接近印象派

Continuing Our Discussion of Boredom and Ennui

And so we must continue our discussion of boredom and ennui
Boring things are all so very
Boring
And any old boring thing is boring too
Only boring things are actually boring
Boredom doesn't need to be discovered it simply is

A sort of remote yet limpid sensation
A certain frenzy
A nostalgia and tremulous sentiment
Not all that far in fact from morality

So how would you describe the taste of boredom?
Only the most sophisticated waiter would say
"We cannot describe the taste of oranges,
We can only say there are certain tastes like oranges."

What entrances us is not its architecture
But its paralysis. There is an ambergris.
Amber-tinged. Nor is there any harm in
Comparing it to inept plumbing.
Brown-paper grocery bags.
A city made of recollections, desires, happy chances and mere coincidences
Sewers pursuing their backward course beneath the historical purview

It really is a problem of atmosphere
Boredom and ennui
Verging on the impressionists

在狂喜最薄最薄的邊上
只有光可以表達
每一個時刻移動的光
那奢侈寧靜那逸樂那膩
是那種以為再也不可能醒來的午睡
接近恐怖主義

接近水泥和砂和鐵
用叉子刮著盤底
剩下一些指甲和皮屑

而並不曾意料的
以傢俱店的形式出現的
店名就叫做厭煩與狂喜的

毫不妥協的低調裝飾
卻是所有的椅子都經過設計
到了絕不可能回返的境地
那些櫃子虛掩
接近直覺

它們帶來凝聚和沉溺的晚上
主題是自我的可厭
遺棄的不同形式
屏風的無目的結論
以及燈光暴力猶豫不決的裝飾性

誰比誰正確，或者說
誰比誰遠離直線
誰比誰更激進

At the sheerest threshold of ecstasy
Only light can express
Light in motion at every moment
That *luxe, calme et volupté* blasé
That siesta you imagine you will never awaken from
Verging on terrorism

Verging on cement and sand and iron
Scouring the bottom of a dish with a fork
Leaving behind bits of nail and skin

But what is least expected
Is that it appears in the form of a furniture store
It just so happens is named "Ennui and Ecstasy"

Utterly uncompromising in its low-key embellishment
All chairs surely undergo a process of design
Until they arrive at the point of no-return
Those wardrobes left unclosed
Verging on intuition

Bearing with them the congealing and wallowing night
Our subject is the odiousness of the ego
The differing forms of abandonment
The purposeless conclusion of the ornamental screen
And the irresolute decorativity of the violence of the lamplight

Who is the more sound or shall we say instead
Who has wandered further from the straight and narrow line
Who is the more radical

更富音樂性
更具節慶氣氛
更允許豐富的插圖
和冗長的遊行隊伍

誰更接近一間完美的浴室
誰比較是浴缸
你不能判斷那狂喜或厭煩
誰是軸誰是旋轉

The more musically endowed
Who evinces the more festive air
Accords the more copious illustration
And the longer procession of marchers
Who is on the verge of the perfect bathroom
Who bears more comparison to a tub
How can you know if it is ecstasy or ennui
Who is the axis who the revolution

無人鋼琴

For J.W.

已經離開了
手還留在身上
一台自動鋼琴
無人在彈

在一個長久凝視啓動的
星雲湧動的宇宙海灘

那些擁抱是
如何完成的
那樣光滑的身體像
兩隻海豚的擁抱像兩座冰山
一起滑入火海裡

那些談話是如何開始的
如此顯得那些根本
不知所以的城市是那麼正確地
完美地對蹠
過那些路過

談話是爲了忽然感到最好還是擁抱
擁抱是爲了可以一起下樓散步
隨便經過一個電影院就買票
進去看電影爲了知道擁抱比電影強大

爲了一再肯定過的
同時並存的許多時間中的
一個就顯得比其他時間
更爲清楚

Playerless Piano

For J. W.

Gone
Still I feel those fingers
On my flesh like the slow glissando
Of a playerless piano

A lingering gaze
Carries us to some unearthly
Shingle surging with clouds of stars

How did we complete
Those caresses
Our naked bodies glistening
Like two dolphins embracing like two glaciers
Slipping into a sea of fire

How did we ever fall into conversation
Thus rendering those accidental cities
We happened to be passing through
So precisely so consummately
Antipodal

We converse so we will know that to embrace is best
And we embrace so we can descend the stairs together
Saunter by a theater and casually buy our tickets
Enter to see a show so we will know
We are mightier than the silver screen

So we will know that among the many
Here and nows we have time and again
Confirmed do coexist there is one which
Stands out clearer than the rest

Tango

輕煙迷漫裡一條船她住在
船艙裡寫她的言情恐怖小說
恐怖是主題言情是裝飾
後來言情的支線逐漸發展恐怖的
氣氛逐漸消滅

順著內陸綿長的河漂流每經過
一個城鎮她下船郵寄她的連載
小說補充糧食日用品遇到喜歡的人
就邀請他們上船敘述生平所遇
最煽情又最恐怖的經歷有人才氣
不夠有人靈感不足她就把他們
騙到船邊在河深處溺斃

言情部份發展出炫耀性的背德片
斷每完成一個段落她對她想像
中的偷窺者說「schmilblick avance」
在晃盪的船艙內她的字往左右傾斜
主題像液體流動枝節蔓衍人物無
故失蹤對話失去線索她上岸去
看牙醫

在牙醫處最新一期「偷窺者」通訊
上她訂了一套百科全書她不時
邀請陌生人上船勒索故事而後
溺斃他們

Scenario for a Tango

Our story opens on a converted river barge lost in mist
Where we find our protagonist who makes this barge her home
Hard at work on a romantic horror thriller
She had started out to write a sort of "Grand Guignol"
But the romantic interests of the story wound up
Taking over until the air of horror
All but disappeared

Drifting down the long inland waterways she often docks at some
Little town or other to post the new installments of her novel
(Did I mention it was a serial?) or replenish her stores or stories
And every time she runs across someone who strikes her fancy
She invites them to join her on the river where she pries from them
Their most passionate and terrifying experience
But whenever the storytellers start to bore her she lures them to the railing
And drowns them in the river where the water runs deep

Now and then her story drifts into shamelessly racy waters
But each time she manages to pilot a chapter safely into port
She turns to that imagined voyeur with a "*Schmilblick avance!*"
And so moving on we find her vessel listing in the waves until
Her words incline to sweeping themes her story is set adrift
Conversations left piled upon the rocks characters lost at sea
And we cut to terra firma to find our heroine
Fairly hurrying to the dentist

Close-up of the writer sitting in a dental waiting room
Filling out an order form for an encyclopedia she found
Flipping through the latest issue of *Voyeur*
Any moment may find her tempting the unsuspecting

那些人消失在她的小說中連河裡也
找不到屍首小說完成時船在
濃霧中儼如鬼船無數說不出
一個完整言情恐怖故事的幽靈圍
在船邊替她打槳用強大的
口氣爲她鼓脹風帆

抒情探戈裡的暗殺裝置　細緻的描寫
引她進入邪途　她穿著狼人裝
在河口遠望　那河已經如此嫻熟
那些失足落水前的吃驚以及她
的倒影　那倒影看起來是狼的
發出狼的聲音她躲在狼裡
用淒厲的音調求偶

Stranger to step on board to tell their tale unless of course . . .
But then we are familiar with her modus operandi

Even the river can find neither head nor heels of
All those people she literally wrote off but
When her tale is done her boat emerges from the spectral fog
And the spirits of those many artless storytellers gather round
Lay hands to oars and with one great breath fill her sails
And set her craft in motion

How the many murderous devices authored in this all-too-lyrical tango
Have lead our heroine off the straight and narrow to the mouth
Of this river where in the guise of a wolf she gazes out into the offing
And we track to the familiar face of the water in which once again we
See those astonished victims drowning in her inverted reflection
As it morphs into the very image of a wolf
Howling for its mate

寫給別人

我在他的手心上寫字筆劃繁複
到成其為勾引而且還寫錯了
又擦掉重寫一橫一豎
一捺一撇勾勒摩擦引他
進入一個象形皮筏裡我把
皮筏的氣放掉我們沉入
湖裡我說我愛你
沒有根也沒有巢
我愛你我愛你把速度
放慢到最慢慢到乃
聽見齒輪滑動旋轉
的聲音在我們身上
一束筒狀的光是誰
發明的電影只是為了讓屋子
暗下來讓我們學會
用慢動作做愛在最慢裡
我愛你慢慢
分解粒子變粗我愛你
我們就轉而無限
分割變細啊我愛你
我愛你
我們變成了自己的陌生人
為了有人以為
他們已經把我們看穿

Written for Others

I write a Chinese character in the palm of his hand
Making it as intricate as I can in the interest of
Arousing his interest I write it wrong so I can rub
It out and write it right from scratch stroke by stroke
Drawing him into one pictographic raft after another
Until I let the air out of the raft and we sink
Into the lake until I say I love you
With neither root nor branch nor a nest to rest
I love you I love you and then I slow us down
Until we barely move at all until we come to hear
The very mesh of the gears turning upon our flesh
There is a cone of light that bares the fact that whoever
Invented the motion picture did so just so we could turn
Down the lights and learn to make love like this
In slow motion and in the slowest possible motion
I love you as we slowly
Dissolve into grains of light I love you
Until we are turning wafer thin
Without end O I love you
I love you
Until we come to be strangers to ourselves
So that others will come to imagine
They have seen through us

我還是願意偷偷自己是那沙丘
被某個晚上的狂風捲走
第2天早上成爲另一種形狀
我也同意我們必須行動
然後在行動裡找到動機
像許多女人會愛上的切‧格瓦拉說的
我穿上印有他頭像的T恤睡覺
對那種再也愛不到的男人只能如此
真想去摸摸他的頭髮
替他點一根煙
爲他找治氣喘的草藥
革命我懂一點
沼澤的水淹沒長征的膝蓋
他愛的唐吉訶德我也懂
與他同一時代的加洛克在路上我也懂
同樣的事物逼近我
用不同的形式
我是切‧格瓦拉今天早上在鏡子裡
我把T恤脫到一半
那頭像罩住了我的臉
露出一隻獨眼
盯住這罕見的一刻
我是那人而那人並不知道
別人也不知道（這些要問波赫士）
我正要解放整個南美
而且我說出了我早已學習準備好
的西班牙文，我只會一句
也是引自波赫士：

Salsa

And still I have this secret yearning to be that sand dune
Swept away one evening by a desert storm
Only to return the following morning in another form
And I agree we must take action and in action
Find our motivation as the much-loved Ché Guevara
To his many *compañera* was often apt to say
I sleep in a T-shirt with his portrait emblazoned on it
And when I think of all those men one can never love again
I long to run my fingers through his hair
Light his cigar
Discover, once and for all, the herbal cure for his asthma
I know a little something of revolution
Knees that have known the long march with the outlaws of the marsh
I know a little something of the Don Quixote that he loved
The Kerouac he packed with him whenever he was on the road
These same things press in upon me
And so I take another form
I am Ché Guevara in the mirror this morning
Slipping my T-shirt halfway off
I find his face covering my own
And I peer through a gap in the cloth
To take in this rare and precious moment
When, like something out of Borges,
I am him and he is unaware that I am him
Nor is anyone aware
Aye mi Cuba, O my Latin America, I come to liberate you
And let me say to you moreover that of the Spanish
I pored over all those many years ago
The only line I can recall (this too from the book of Borges) is
My destiny lies in the Spanish language.

「我的命運在西班牙文裡」
但是我接著說　　用他不懂的中文：
「我跟你一起去革命
但是允許我隨時可以逃走」
這首詩這麼膚淺
不免被所有人恥笑
但根據波赫士
所有寫好的詩
都早已經有它們的位置
它早已存在
早於所有的革命
以及我的逃走
關於革命和詩彼此傾軋的部份
我播放一段 salsa 跳舞打混過去

Or as I meant to say: *Mi destino es la lengua castellana.*
"I will go with you to the revolution,
But you must give me your permission
To desert you should I feel the need arise"
But I shouldn't wonder if the shallowness of my verse
Has reduced everyone to jeers
But then again if you have read your Borges
You should know that it was always already there
In every revolution
In my every desertion
And as for the part where poetry and revolution jostle each other
I'll put on a *salsa* or two to help me muddle through

太初有字

桓公曰然則有鬼乎曰有沈有履灶有髻戶
內之煩壤雷霆處之東北方下者倍阿鮭蠪
躍之西北方之下者則泆陽處之水有罔象
丘有峷山有夔野有彷徨澤有委蛇
莊子達生第十九

1
想像從來沒有什麼過般地愛你
而且很想向你顯示軟弱
所愛上的你包括所沒有愛上的你
而奇怪的是也只不過更加
「回到自己」甚至也懂得了
你還不懂得的我的那一面所
懂得的你

2
也曾用書寫的虛無引誘過你
那些鬼影幢幢的字五千年
掀不完一層又一層轉世的靈魂
來到筆尖
等待一個新的意志附身

3
那些字
其實它們早就先到
又不著痕跡地回來
讓人領它們前去

In the Beginning was the Written Word

> *And the Duke of Huan asked: "But are there really ghosts?" "Indeed, there are," was the reply: "In the hearth one finds the Lu and in the oven the Ji. And among the rubbish heaped outside the city gate the Leiting makes its home. And in the northeast corner the Beia and the Gueilung make sport, and in the northwest corner the Yiyang dwells. And in the water lurks the Wangxiang; on the hills, the Shen; in the mountains, the Kuei; in the pastures, the Fanghuang; and in the marshes, the Weiyi."*
> The Book of Zhuangzi, Chapter 19: "Mastering Life"

1

I wish that I had never loved anyone as I love you
And I want so very much to reveal to you my frailty
The part of you I love includes the part of you I don't
And strangely enough this only seems to have
"Returned me to myself" as they say and so much so
I have even come to understand you have yet to understand
The part of me that understands you

2

I have at times seduced you with the emptiness of the word
The ghostly procession haunting us these 5000 years
Never an end to their unfolding
Generation after generation
Alighting on the tips of our pens
To wait for some new will on which to feed

3

But actually these words are always arriving before us
Returning each time as pristine as ever
Waiting for us to lead them on

4
「我喚他
他回答　是　怎麼樣
我說　沒事　只想確定你在
他並不常存在
我也是　不常
有些稀有時刻
剛好都在
就慎重地稱之爲愛」

5
我們是被這些字所發生的嗎
此事如果又指向另一些事——
我們暱稱的萬物萬事
有時候我贊成用我崇拜的睡眠代表憐憫

6
當然有另外一些字
從來沒有等到過任何
可以嵌入的情況
也無以理解它們是不是在等待
等待像我這樣的人
強制它們變成一首詩的開頭

7
那些詩
我發現它們會隨著光線變化
像貓眼

8
那些貓
牠們一再藏匿
牠們也會挨近
當牠們確實樂意

4

"I called out to him
And he answered: 'Yeh, what's up?'
'Nothing,' I said. 'I only wanted to know if you were there.'
He is not often there you know
Me neither for that matter
But we have our rare moments when we both are
Moments we gingerly call 'Love'"

5

Have words invented us?
And does this point to other things as well —
"The ten thousand things" as they are called?
Sometimes I praise them by letting the sleep I so worship
Intercede for my deficiency of sympathy

6

And of course there are those words
That have never waited for any situation
To insinuate themselves into
Nor can we ever be sure if they are even waiting
Waiting like me like this
To force them into the genesis of
A poem

7

And these poems I discover
Are always changing with the light
Like the eye of a cat

8

And these cats
Are always scurrying off
Although sometimes they will approach you
When they feel like meandering over

美好邪惡往日

神造世界第 7 天大家又懶又不愛了
在林子裡遊蕩
滿溢的存在在
雨後的馬糞上長出牛肝菌
大家分頭在森林裡找牛肝菌
牛肝菌採回來
洗乾淨，稍微泡軟
在小火裡乾煸出水
煎以牛油
施以蒜末香芹
佐以烘軟的乾酪和
鄉下火腿薄片

此時氣氛屬於美好邪惡往日
各種舊椅墊般舒適
的心裡危機　泛黃的精緻的鏤空的
蕾絲的花邊裝飾著的各式各類的
倒行逆施的容器裡保持的怪癖
開一瓶八七年的波爾多無伴奏
但也被控為同謀
之後就失去連絡但是
把怪僻部份
當做默契帶走

Those Gloriously Sinful Days of Old

God made the heaven and the earth and on the seventh day languid and
No longer loving we drifted into the forest
So brimming with existence after the rain
There were porcini growing in the horse manure
And we separated in search of more
And when we had found some we took them home
And washed them off and soaked them till they were soft and tender
And braised them over a low flame until the juices ran
And fried them gently in butter
And garlic and celery
And dressed them with toasted cheese
And slivers of prosciutto

And for a moment the ambience belonged to those gloriously sinful days of old
The psychological crises we sank into like so many sofa chairs
In exquisite lacework covers flower-fringed and yellowed
The many eccentricities we preserved in our perverse and sundry vessels
And we decanted an '87 Bordeaux and nursed it a capella
But then our complicity was brought to light
And we fell out of touch
But not before carrying away those eccentricities
That serve as our tacit understanding

開車到里斯本

難免有旅館裡住著暴露狂
如果難免也有隱匿狂的話
整個旅館的外觀提供的幻覺
必須視毒品的種類或酒精的
強度決定而由此界定的
現實又讓人產生極端誠懇
或極端不誠懇之感亦或是
過於嫻熟或不夠嫻熟之類的
不好意思於是我說服了她
接受孤獨知道這事是甚至
乃值得喜愛但不久我就發現她愛的

孤獨乃是我的孤獨而不是
她自己的孤獨她那麼愛我的孤獨
急欲加入所以我們就一起開車
到里斯本看一個我們都
喜歡的朋友那人也有他的孤獨
但是他管它叫
我的母鹿。

Driving Down to Lisbon

If certain hotels happen to have these exhibitionists
Because they also have these hyper-reclusive types
Then the illusion generated by the entire hotel façade
Hinges on the intensity of the alcohol or the class
Of drug used and so the ensuing reality
Makes for these feelings of extreme sincerity or
Extreme insincerity or the embarrassment of
Being too familiar with something or not
Familiar enough and when I had finally persuaded her to
Accept the loneliness to accept this thing as something
Even worthy of her love I soon came to realize

The loneliness she had come to love was mine and not
Her own and she had such a fierce desire
To join it that we drove down to
Lisbon to see a friend we all liked
And he had his loneliness too
But he called it
My mother deer my doe.

自我的地獄

致波赫士

一堆夢遊者與另一堆夢遊者
擦身而過他們的夢有所交集
像幾塊雲遇到另幾塊雲
就下了一場雨其中的一個
夢遊者醒在一個屋子裡
他睜開眼睛說：下雨了
完全不知道自己夢遊過
而且醒在別人的屋子裡
他的腳在別人的鞋裡
是那麼吻合他的身體穿上
別人的衣服他坐在另一個
桌子前與另一些人一起吃飯
他變成另一個我且不疑有他
朋友或配偶可能也懷疑過
但被存在本質上更虛幻的疑點
所說服在這裡鞋子
是關鍵穿錯鞋子
很容易就會發現不是嗎此所以
每個早上所有起床的人
首先被他們自己的鞋子說服
從不懷疑他們已經
不是他們自己奇怪的是
別人的鞋子為什麼會合
自己的腳呢因為只要有一個人
沒有醒來大家就全部
活在他的夢裡

A Personal Hell

To Borges

When sleepwalkers chance to
Come across each other their dreams
Intermingle like two clouds converging
And it rains and one of the sleepers
Wakes inside a room and
Opens his eyes and says: "It is raining"
Never knowing that his nocturnal wanderings have landed him in
Some other person's home wearing some other person's shoes
Which for some odd reason fit as snuggly as his own
Wearing some other person's clothes sitting down to breakfast
At some other person's table with some other person's significant other
Never knowing that he himself has become an other
And while there are surely some among his friends and family
Who have come to harbor certain vague suspicions that he is not
The person he appears to be nothing ever comes of this
As such suspicions seem part of the general irreality
Nor will he ever come to know that it is the shoes that sustain the illusion
For wouldn't you know if the shoes you were wearing were not your own?
Thus are we each persuaded every morning when we rise
Won over by the shoes and the rest it never occurs to us
We are no longer quite ourselves
And the uncanny part of this is that
The reason why other people's shoes
Always seem to fit so well is that as long as
There is but one of us still fast asleep
The rest of us live on inside the dream

帶一籃水果去看她

今天我去一個地方有人告訴我下次不要再來了／我
告訴他反正我也不想去了／有人會去但那是另一回
事／我回到租來的公寓蒸一條魚／一個朋友來和我
一起吃魚／吃完魚他說他最近不好／丟了工作／又
錯過一班火車南下找工作／那些工作都花力氣花精
神花光所有的存在他說／然後你就分期付款買房子
和買車子然後找到一個女人／你們生一些小孩小孩
長得太像你不好意思不像你也不好意思／我們講了
一下當房東和房客的差別／然後我們就做了／他問
你有幾個愛人我有什麼不一樣／我說廢話你當然不
一樣／他堅持問那裡不一樣／我說你就是不一樣如
果你一定要知道那裡不一樣我只好說好吧你沒什麼
不一樣／你看我就知道他說／你反正等最壞的我說
／對這樣我就安靜了他說／我們一起看錄影帶人魚
公主／人魚公主失去聲音的時候他哭了／我們不斷
倒帶看我們喜歡的段落／又蒸一條魚吃／我把塔羅
牌翻開看他會不會找到工作及看看我們會怎麼樣／
你找不到工作的我說／啊找不到嗎他說／對試也不
用試／那我怎麼辦／沒怎麼辦你會比較安靜我說／
那我們會結婚嗎他問／也不會我說／牌不準他說我
怎麼知道它說的是真的／你是不知道我說我也無法
讓你知道／那你爲什麼相信它／就在我把牌翻開的
那一秒鐘我說開天關地以來所有的因果關係都暗中
自行推算加減了一翻／少來宇宙那一套他說／如果
宇宙不是這樣一套我們就不會坐在這裡玩牌我說／

Taking Her a Basket of Fruit

Today I go to a place and some guy there tells me not to come any more/ I tell him I didn't feel like going there anyway/ Maybe others do but that's another matter/ So I go back to the flat I'm renting and steam a fish/ A friend drops by and we eat the fish/ When we finish the fish he says he hasn't been feeling too chipper lately/ Lost his job/ Missed his train to look for another one down south/ Those jobs just eat you alive he says/ You get a mortgage buy a house a car get yourself a woman/ You make some kids and if they look too much like you you feel embarrassed/ And if they don't look anything like you you feel just as embarrassed/ So then we talk awhile about the differences between being a landlord and a tenant/ Then we do it/ He asks how many lovers you have and am I any different/ What a stupid question I say of course you're different/ So he asks me how am I different/ I say you're just different that's all and if you really want to know maybe you're not so different after all/ You can tell that just by looking at me he says/ You're so weird always waiting for the worst to happen/ But then when it does I can settle down he says/ We look at *The Little Mermaid* on the VCR/ When the little mermaid loses her voice he cries/ We keep rewinding to the parts we like/ Steam another fish/ I lay out the Tarot cards to check out his job prospects and see if there's any kind of future for us in the cards/ Well you're not going to find a job I say/ I'm not he says/ No point in even looking/ So what do I do/ There's nothing you can do but at least you can settle down now that you know the worst/ So do the cards say we'll get married or something he asks/ Doesn't look that way I say/ The cards are off he says and how do you know what the cards say is true anyway/ You don't know what I'm saying so there's no way I can make you understand what I'm talking about/ So why do you believe in them/

我有點膩了我又說我想搬家了／那你翻一張看看你找不找得到房子他說／牌翻開／牌說我找得到房子／那你再問它我可不可以跟你一起住他說／牌說不可以／我們又做了一次／反正不知道做什麼好／然後他走了／我再也沒有看見過他從此以後／可能還有別的結論但是我還不知道／另一個朋友打電話來說唉我真的不知道他愛不愛我／他愛的我說／你怎麼知道她說／因為他不愛我我說／她掛了電話／我又把牌翻開／我知道等一下她還會打電話問那你愛不愛他／果然她打來了／我說愛因為想讓她生氣／我知道她會馬上打電話問他她愛你為什麼你不愛她／她等著他說我愛她／她也在等最壞的／然後她就安靜了／因為反正大家都不愛她／她疲倦極了／我們也是／後來我就搬家了／沒有帶一籃水果去看她

I believe in them I say because the split second before I flip the cards over I know all the cause and effect relations since the universe began secretly work themselves out to like the final permutation/ Enough of this universe shit he says/ If it weren't for this universe shit we wouldn't be lying here reading the cards/ I'm a little fed up so I say I'm thinking of moving anyway/ Well why don't you ask the cards and see if you'll find a place/ I turn a card over/ It says I will/ Well then ask them if I can move in with you he says/ The cards say no way/ We do it again/ We didn't know what else to do/ He leaves/ And I never see him again/ Maybe it will all play out differently one day but right now I just don't know/ Then another friend calls me up and says I really don't know if he loves me or not/ He loves you I say/ How do you know she says/ Because he doesn't love me I say/ She hangs up/ I lay the cards out again/ I know that if I wait a little while she'll call me back and ask do you love him/ Sure enough she calls back/ I say I love him just to make her jealous/ I know she'll call him as soon as she hangs up and say if she loves you why don't you love her/ She'll wait for him to say but I do love her/ She's always waiting for the worst too/ But later on she'll settle down/ Because nobody loves her anyway/ She's pretty fed up with it all/ And so are we/ Later I move/ And I never do take her a basket of fruit

拿一把扇子正面畫一隻鳥
反面畫一個鳥籠
快速轉動扇柄就看到
一隻鳥被關在籠子裡她
把扇子收起來她
微笑著要大家猜那是什麼意思

我們說我愛你她說不對
於是我們說我不愛你還是不對然後
她就帶我們去她的公寓

蟑螂在朝北的老舊的公寓裡繁殖
她啟示我們牠們繁殖產卵的地方
傳真機的底盤
答錄機的錄音座
電視裡的管子隙縫
那些用電長期熱著的地方
我們懂了什麼吧恐怕也沒有

我們只是滿想也這樣鑽進
音響裡和她　　賴在音樂流出來
的地方不起床　　在所有那些我們稱之為
時代的局限的早上大家是
多麼多麼地目眩神搖
讓彼美好事物相遇吧
讓痛苦給予力量吧任何時候
讓我們指著自己身上瘀青的部份

Somehow

She took a fan and painted a bird on one side
And a cage on the other and then she spun
The handle in her hand till we could see the bird
In the cage and then she put the fan away and smiling
Asked us what we thought it was she'd said

I love you we said but that was wrong she said and then
We said I love you not but that was wrong
As well and then she took us home

Roaches flourish in these aging north-facing flats
She enlightened us as to the many places they infest
The belly of the fax machine
The interstices of the TV
The tape well of the answering machine
All those places warmed the year long by electricity
Did we have any conception? No, not really

All that we could think of was how nice it would be
If we too could worm our way into the hi-fi with her
And make our indolent bed there where the music pours out
On all those mornings which we dub the limitations of the age
When we are reeling in the radiance we say
Let all good things converge
Let our pain be our strength and at any moment let us
Be prepared to show our guests the bruises on our hips
And the scratches on our backs as we recite those
Words from somewhere "*L'amour n'existe pas,*
Mais la preuve d'amour existe"

對接著來訪的客人引用一句
那裡抄來的話愛不存在
可是愛的證據存在
任何時候我們去她的房間
那混亂都像小偷剛來過
最後小偷也終於來了
她與小偷之間的共謀是
他拿走了她不需要的東西所以她並不知道他拿走了
重要的是他幫她翻出了她久久失散尋找之物
所以之後任何時候
我們進去她的房間
她有一種「被怎麼折疊都可以」的表情

Every time we went to her flat it had that look
Of having been ransacked by thieves and
Indeed a thief did finally pay a call
And the conspiracy they hatched was this
He took only things she did not need so she never knew he took them
More importantly he helped her rummage up the things she'd lost
And so then whenever we went to her flat she wore a
"Just fold me any which way" look

初級氣氛

不愛了但仍然值得一切的榮耀
把他們裝在不同的船上送走
留下我們的小孩
被一些穀倉的乾草堆
一些雨季一堆無恥的誓言
各式絕無僅有的現在
所發明出來的小孩

但我猜我們所看見的這些小孩
都已經被偷偷地交換過了
被就是「偷偷交換」這個想法

和傘一樣
或者打火機
有人盜火
有人偷書
有人幹盆景

誰正好偷到了什麼就應該好好照顧
但是偷之前或偷之後
有一個短暫的中途忘了偷這件事
而且不喜歡大家偷來偷去

被偷過的小孩有一種氣氛
不知道對什麼的不屑
總要面臨
而最終也了悟了的
「相對地有限」

Entry-Level Aura

No longer loving yet not unworthy of our praise and honor
Let me pack them off on different ships
Leaving behind our children
Those inventions of so many singular here and
Nows born of haylofts voluptuous
Rains and shameless
Vows

But I imagine the children we see before us
Have long been switched under our very eyes
"Secretly interchanged" by the very thought itself

Like so many umbrellas
Or lighters
Someone once stole fire
Others are always stealing books
Others yet are into scoring potted landscapes

Whoever happens to run off with something ought to take care of it at least
But then there's always a moment or two in the course of a theft
When you forget you're stealing something and on top of that
Can't really stand all this stealing going on

Stolen children have an aura about them
A certain disdain you can't quite put your finger on
But sooner or later must come face to face with
Until you arrive in the end at a sudden revelation of
"The relatively limited"

但小孩是自動繁殖的
經過一扇自動門被夾了一下
一個小孩就變成兩個小孩
這是據我們所不知的

他們遠比我所能想像的還更不重視
父親這回事而且想盡辦法
找出我的不在場證明

但是一開始的一開始呢
當我這樣發問我知道
我只是想讓他們把
作業寫好而且只是極個人地
喜歡一切入門的初級氣氛

我早早吵醒他們
就好像要一起去偷車
又好像要在另一個清晨一起離去

But children are self-propagating creatures
Pinched between a pair of automatic doors
A child will turn into two children
But all this lies in the horizon of our ignorance

How they value this thing called fatherhood so much
Less than I can imagine and how hard they work
To muster alibis to prove I was never at the scene

And at the beginning of the beginning?
But I've no sooner asked this than I know
All I really want is for them to finish their homework and
Know moreover the enjoyment I find in all this elementary
Entry-level aura is wholly peculiar to me

I rouse them up in the wee hours of the morning
As if we were off to steal a car
Or as if it were some other early morning we were running off together

Fusion Kitsch

什麼時候開始的
這牧歌式的泛亂倫氣氛
那早就屬於同一本家庭相本的
已經淪落爲親人的愛人們
那些淪落爲愛人的動物們
還有所有羅曼史最終到達
之萬物有靈論述
裡的壓抑傾向

Fusion Kitsch

When did it all begin
This bucolic and pan-incestuous atmosphere
Was it not always there in the selfsame family album
Lovers fallen to the status of kin
Animals fallen to the condition of lovers
Nor let us forget the repressive inclinations
In the animistic discourse to which
All romances arrive in the end

● 摩擦 ● 無以名狀

FROM *RUB: INEFFABLE* (1995)

● 我們小心養大的水銀

穿過
黑色鞦韆廢墟
滲出邊界
延長舞蹈
逼近肉體邊廂
清晨6時
出了暗淡的月

The Mercury We So Carefully Raise

passing through
the ruins of the black see-saw
oozing out of the borderlands
prolonging the dance
pressing upon the chambers of the flesh
early morning 6 A.M.
tendering the pale moon

● 閱讀

舌尖上
一隻蟹

Reading

a crab
on the tip of the tongue

● 舌頭

清晰地
　厭世
在洞裡
冷淡遲疑恐怖
抗拒的鱷魚

Tongue

clearly
world-weary
in its hole
cold irresolute fearsome
defiant crocodile

● 明信片

時間不多
謹慎的小城
不無互相毀滅
即將遠走
打破玻璃
指甲透明

Carte Postale

so little time
little city of circumspection
not above a mutual destruction
on the verge of a long voyage
the breaking of the glass
translucent as a fingernail

● 八項

四月微冰的海水
昔日談情的樓窗
　　粗糙的折磨
　　看電影的人
每一個人的分配
　　　我的自私
　　長久的睡眠
反射著彼此的光

Octet

the slightly icy April seawater
those storied windows where in former days we spoke of love
coarse trials and afflictions
moviegoers
the allotment of each of us
my selfishness
a long sleep
light that we reflect upon each other

● 紫色地下

當這樣埋著深埋著的時候
就感覺左邊的肩膀慢慢
濕潤變
紫可以說：是的，我
願意。

Purple Underground

when buried so completely so deeply
I can feel my very clavicle
growing moist and
purple till I say: I
will. I
do

● 摩擦 ● 無以名狀

貓咪　今天　聽到
你叫我　回到　一個
廝混的　巴洛克式
的了解　貓咪　問題
是　我的　遺忘
像　幽靈　我的
罪惡　像　歌劇　我
的　失　眠　遠足
曠野　問　題　是
貓咪　我的　旋轉
如果　是　無謂
我的柔軟　是
那個　惋惜　我　的
溫暖　是　這個
游離　貓咪
我的　閃爍　我的　撞擊
就是　牠
最愛　的　魚

Rub: Ineffable

Puss   today   I heard you
calling me   returning   me
to our baroque   and promiscuous under-
standing   Puss   the problem
is   just this   that my forgetfulness
is   so much   like a specter   my
sins   the very image of   an opera   my
sleeplessness   sallies
to a wilderness   afar   the problem
Puss   is this   that if all my   gyrations
are   so very   senseless
then my softness   is
that   very pity   my
warmth   in fact   that
very distance   Puss
my   luster   and my   skittish buffeting
are nothing   other than
your   favorite   fish

腹語術

FROM *VENTRILOQUY* (1991)

腹語術

我走錯房間
錯過了自己的婚禮。
在牆壁唯一的隙縫中，我看見
一切行進之完好。　她穿白色的外衣
她捧著花，儀式，
許諾，親吻
背著它：命運，我苦苦練就的腹語術
（舌頭那匹溫暖的水獸　馴養地
在小小的水族箱中　蠕動）
那獸說：是的，我願意。

Ventriloquy

I walk into the wrong room
And miss my own wedding.
Through the only hole in the wall I see
All proceeding perfectly: The groom in white
The bride with flowers in her hand, the rites
The vows, the kiss
Turning my back on it: fate, the ventriloquy
I've worked so long and hard at
(tongue, that warm aquatic creature,
squirms domestic in its tank)
And the creature says: I do.

隱匿的王后和她不可見的城市

在她的國度，一張
牽強附會的地圖。
出走的銅像不被履行的
遺書和諾言識破的陷阱
混淆的線索和消滅中的指紋以及
所有遺失的眼鏡和傘等
組成的國度。
她暗中畫著虛線，無限
擴大的版圖。
一座分類詳盡的失物博物館，好極了。
另外呢，就是那些命運以及
歷史都還未曾顯現跡象的時刻吧
她草擬了秋天的徒步計劃（目的不明
但將在每一個十字路口右轉）
寫好了一個輕歌劇
餵了貓
寫了信
打一個蝴蝶結
在永不悔悟的心

The Cloistered Queen and Her Invisible City

In the kingdom of our cloistered queen
There is a map drawn in many a forced analogy.
A kingdom cobbled out of vagrant bronzes, broken
Promises and testaments, pitfalls that have fallen through
Befuddling clues, obliterated fingerprints
And every parasol and pair of glasses ever lost.
It is a vast and limitless domain
Whose imaginary lines
She traces in the dark. A veritable
Fully catalogued *Musée des objets perdues—C'est formidable*!
And? Nothing less than those moments of our destinies and
Our histories whose signs have yet to be revealed.
Having drafted her plan for an Autumn amble (destination unknown
as yet but entailing a right turn at every crossing)
She puts the final touches to her opera
Feeds the cat
Pens a letter
And ties a bow in the
Unrepentant heart

（非常緩慢而且甜蜜的死）

天使試著發現自己。他們不相信深奧。
雖然他們擁有全套的潛水裝備。
這麼容易入睡。
他們洗一個澡，當有人要求
爲「完整的救贖」舉例的時候
我肉體邊廂的幽靈
我們和天使的區別是
我們的沸點不同
他們容易蒸發
而且比較傾向於愛。
雖然我們也是這麼這麼的透明
卻被各種邪惡的枝節感動啓發
帶著大大的悲傷醒來
並在不斷叉開的故事支線上
走失了我們唯一的那隻羊

(*A Sweet and Lingering Death*)

The angels endeavor to discover who they are. They profess no faith in depth.
Notwithstanding their possession of the necessary diving gear.
To slip so easily into sleep.
They bathe, for the moments they are called upon to furnish
Instances of "absolute redemption"
My soul inhabiting the chambers of the flesh
What distinguishes the angels from us is
The difference in our boiling points
They evaporate more readily and are more inclined to love.
Notwithstanding our possession of a copious transparency
Aroused by vicious complications
We wake to our heavy load of sorrow
While on the forking branches of the tale
We have lost our only lamb

頽廢末帝國

給秋瑾

不無互相毀滅可能的華爾滋
　　　　如你的革命

我發現我以男裝出現
　　　　　如你

　　　舞至極低
　　極低的無限

　　即將傾倒
一個潰爛的王朝

但我只不過是雌雄同體
　在幽暗的沙龍裡

　　　釋放著華美
　　高亢的男性

L'Empire à la Fin de la Décadence

For Qiu Jin, Qing dynasty revolutionary martyr

A waltz not without its possibilities of mutual destruction
Like your revolution

I discover I've appeared in the guise of a man
Like you

Dancing toward the nadir
Nadir *ad infinitum*

To the endless verge of toppling
The empire at the end of its decadence

But I am merely an androgyne
In a gloomy *salon*

Releasing my splendor
My clamorous masculinity

重金屬

想像他們帶著牠們行走
在路上遇到朋友
他們也許互相嫉妒而牠們並不
他們互相比較
不，她們並不常討論牠們
僅以某種柔軟空洞自喜
當牠們在她們隱密的地方
見證一種鋼的脆弱
而又愉悅了她們
她們想像他們帶著牠們行走
在路上遇到朋友
牠們互相嫉妒
而他們並不

Heavy Metal

Imagine men lugging their tools around with them
Bumping into their friends on the street
And becoming a little jealous even
As they size each other up
But no — women do not often talk of tools
Their pleasure is reserved for those soft and empty boxes
That bear witness to the frailty of steel
And give them such delight
When the tools are nestled in their secret compartments
Women imagine men lugging their tools around with them
Bumping into their friends on the street
And the tools becoming a little jealous even
Rather than the men

十四首十四行之五首

時間如水銀落地

好像一切都還沒有開始
在海　或是銅板的反面。
衣櫃後的牆　牆上的洞　洞的深處
五月晨光裡的第一道褶縫。　　床
床底下鋪滿他們的智齒
從一本裝錯封面且永不被發現
的書裡的插圖中走了出來
做出深思熟慮以及我還有很多時間的微笑
初夏的棉布裙被潑翻的葡萄柚汁打溼
在另一個可能的過去
我的眼睛曾是黃昏最疲憊的商旅
耳環傾斜了存在
慾望反著光
時間如水銀落地

And time falls like mercury

As if nothing had yet begun
In the sea or on the flip-side of the coin.
On the wall behind the highboy, in the hole in the wall, in the depths of the hole
The first fold in the morning light of May. The bed
The growing mound of wisdom teeth beneath the bed
Stepping from an illustration in a book
No one ever will discover was bound in the wrong cover
Making that smile when I am deep in thought with all the time in the world
A cotton summer dress soiled through some carelessness with fruit juice
In another possible past
My eyes have been a haggard caravan at day's end
An earring tipping this existence in recline
When desire reflects the light
And time falls like mercury

在另一個可能的過去

在另一個可能的過去
他或許也曾如此逼近
而我迂迴地倒退著走
回到了謹慎開始的那一個房間
邊界緩緩移動向無可臆度的黑暗
房間如細胞分裂增殖
所有的門虛掩著　所有的外套解開了
第一個鈕扣　所有的水龍頭漏著水
在深夜　　口袋裡藏著指甲
和故事的碎片
我們小心養大的水銀終於打碎了
滾落四處
每一滴都完整自足
我們何不像水銀　分手

In another possible past

In another possible past
He may have also pressed this close
And I, meandered back to
That room of guarded beginnings.
The borderlands inch their way toward the immeasurable darkness.
The room divides and multiplies like replicating cells.
In every room a door is left cracked open. On every coat a button left
Undone. Every faucet drips through
The middle of the night. As our pockets fill with fingernails
And fragments of the tale.
And in the end the mercury we have so carefully raised is shattered
Spawling off in all directions
Each and every drop perfect unto itself
Why aren't we like the mercury when we part

一些一些地遲疑地稀釋著的我

一些一些地遲疑地稀釋著的我
如此與你告別分手
草草約了來生，卻暫時也
還不想死。游離著
分裂著。在所有可能的過去
我們或許也曾這樣陷入於
以訛傳訛的政黨或秘教以及清晨6時
市集裡傾翻的香料
用十匹騾子交換一個廝混的黃昏
你盛裝而慘敗
顛覆了
我最冷淡不祥的感官，傾斜的剎那
我們的相遇只是為了重複相遇的虛無
當死亡的犁騷動著春天的田畝

Gradually diluted with every parting I

Gradually diluted with every parting I
Say goodbye and we go our separate ways
For all our hurried promises of meeting in the next life
For the moment at least I am content to go on
Living in this one. Drifting
Dissipating. Perhaps in every possible past we
Became entangled in a warren of politics and esoteria
Chanced upon the herbs spilled in the agora that early morning 6 am
Bartered a train of mules for a single evening we idled away
And you are dressed in your best and are defeated
Toppling
My indifferent and inauspicious senses, at the inclining instant
Have we met only to rehearse the null and void of meeting
As the fatal plough disturbs the vernal field

在牆上留下一個句子

那些流淚分手的清晨
起床後第一個吻淡綠如梗
對著一面骯髒的鏡子
重新把耳環戴好
在牆上留下一個句子：
「憂鬱底心的暗暗底歡愉。」
我們所錯過的四月微冰的海水和
不能相遇所虛擲的時間
我們所錯過的銅器店正午閃過一張貓的臉
一本導遊手冊叫做「寂寞的星球」
一些船離開港口。一些人從此不再出現。
一種希臘的藍加上一些土耳其的綠。
水瓶裡密封的音樂和染料。以及廢墟。
「你是我最完整的廢墟」

Leaving a sentence on the wall

Those early mornings with their tearful separations
The first kiss after getting out of bed pale green as a stem
Facing a filthy mirror
Putting earrings back in place
Leaving a sentence on the wall:
"The secret joys of the melancholy heart."
The slightly icy April seawater that we missed and
Those wasted hours when by chance we could not meet
The brass shop that we missed where at noon there flashed the face of a cat
A copy of the "Lonely Planet"
Some ships leave the harbor. Some people never appear again.
A certain Grecian blue tinged with Turkish green.
The music and dye sealed within a water bottle. And the ruins.
"You are my most consummate ruin"

我確實在培養著新的困境

回到謹慎開始的那一頁：
我確實在培養著新的困境
發明各種瑣碎的口令和道具而我幾幾
乎只喜歡他們睡著的樣子可他們並不知道
他們辯稱夢見我當我挨近
在他們臉頰上吹氣我的羽翼
在人體上投下網狀的陰影；
關於他們所不能全盤瞭然的
另一個房間裡的一切
關於某種軟弱的動物性關於這時候
你走進來一輛卡車開過反光鏡上
佈滿旅行者衰弱的臉孔你用食指
輕輕畫過我的腳心你說你知道嗎那躺在
床上的你已經死了回來的只是你的靈魂

I find that I am definitely fostering new predicaments

Returning to that page of guarded beginnings:
I find that I am definitely fostering new predicaments
Contriving trivial shibboleths and stage props and I really
Really only like the way they sleep but what do they know of this
Arguing about having dreamt me when I draw near
My wings stirring the air above their cheeks
My shadow casting its net over their sleeping forms;
And as for that which they can never fully know
The all and everything of another room
As for that certain fragile animality as for this moment
You enter as a lorry appears in a rear view mirror filled with
The travelers' weary faces as you lightly trace a finger
Down the arch of my foot saying don't you know the you that is lying
On this bed is dead and the you that has returned is only your soul

早期及未結集之詩

SELECTED EARLY OR UNCOLLECTED POEMS

翻譯

年老的僧侶翻譯著經書
他5就出家了
許多事沒有經歷過
那些陌生的語言像他年輕時
夢見過的身體
他努力遄想那些字的意思　　經年累月地
搜索自己的母語
找出對應的態；
那些身體，他想
只要撫摸過一次——
那身體，被一道強光緊緊包圍著的
令他更懂得了些：
某些字完全無法翻譯
置他於生離死別之境
而他是徒然地老了
翻不出來的
只好自行創作
但最好看起來像翻譯一樣
如果他曾撫摸過
即使穿著雨衣戴著手套

Translation

An aging monk translates a holy book
Having entered the order in childhood
There are many things he has never lived
These exotic tongues
So like the bodies he dreamt of in his youth
He racks his brains to find the meaning of the text and the years gather dust
Rummaging through the nooks and crannies of his mother tongue
In search of those ministering words and phrases
He calls to mind the bodies
He never had the chance to touch
A vision of flesh lit by a fierce and clinching light
Leaves him with this deeper insight:
Certain words will not cross over
But put him in peril of never meeting again
To what avail has he grown old?
Words he cannot translate
He must now invent
But better they give the appearance of translation
If only he had touched them
Even through a pair of gloves
Or a veil for that matter

更多的人願意涉入

其一
一個人搬家後所留出來的空間
就會被另一個想搬家的人佔據
所留出來的空間也就製造出
另一搬家動機以此類推種種
你不愛他就有別人不愛你
的種種 fuckable-
的種種 unfuckable-
所根據歌德萬物包含萬物
萬物與萬物有關與萬物
對應辯證
一同毀滅重生
我們大家與萬物
就都又重新就都又大家
又興奮起來

其二
不愛的時候這些多麼不重要
甚至懶得敘述它們的不重要性
就是一個必須經過的城市
火車停靠讓上車的人上車
下車的人下車我與鄰座的人
保持不動繼續旅行他意識到
他的不重要性是我的賦予
之後不會記得記得了也沒有將就
屬於一切意義連否認
也嫌太多的曾經
某時某刻遇見過又怎麼樣
的我們只是使今後的我們

More and More People Wanting to Get Involved

Variation One

A person picks up house and moves and the space they leave behind
Becomes occupied by someone else
Leaving behind a space that creates in turn
A pretext for yet another to pick up house from which we can analogize so many
If you no longer love him then someone else no longer loves you
So many *fuckable*
So many *unfuckable*
According to Goethe everything contains within itself every other thing
The relationship between all things and all things
Resonating in the dialectic of sympathy and opposition
Coupling destruction and rebirth
Each and every one of us and each and every thing
Is once more renewed and we find ourselves
Growing eager again

Variation Two

When you do not love none of this is the least important
So much so its *un*importance is hardly worth describing
A city you are simply passing through
As the train pulls into the station and some people get on
And others get off and the person sitting next to me
Keeps his seat and as the train begins to move he comes to realize
His unimportance is something I've bestowed
But by and by we will no longer recall this and even if we do it's not likely
To find a ready place within the total significance and even disavowing it
Is hardly worth the trouble so
If at some time and place our paths have crossed what of it
That we will only make the we to come

更不重要我們
根本不重要

其三
一個人搬家後所留出來的空間
不愛的時候這些多麼不重要
就會被另一個想搬家的人佔據
甚至懶得敘述它們的不重要性
所留出來的空間也就製造出
就是一個必須經過的城市
另一搬家動機以此類推種種
火車停靠讓上車的人上車
你不愛他就有別人不愛你
下車的人下車我與鄰座的人
的種種 fuckable-
保持不動繼續旅行他意識到
的種種 unfuckable-
他的不重要性是我的賦予
所根據歌德萬物包含萬物
之後不會記得記得了也沒有將就
萬物與萬物有關與萬物
屬於一切意義連否認
對應辯證
也嫌太多的曾經
一同毀滅重生
某時某刻遇見過又怎麼樣
我們大家與萬物
的我們只是使今後的我們
就都又重新就都又大家
更不重要我們
又興奮起來
根本不重要

All the less important we are
Simply unimportant

Variation Three

A person picks up house and moves and the space they leave behind
When you do not love none of this is the least important
Becomes occupied by someone else
So much so its unimportance is hardly worth describing
Leaving behind a space that creates in turn
A city you are simply passing through
A pretext for yet another to pick up house from which we can analogize so many
As the train pulls into the station and some people get on
If you no longer love him then someone else no longer loves you
And others get off and the person sitting next to me
So many *fuckable*
Keeps his seat and as the train begins to move he comes to realize
So many *unfuckable*
His unimportance is something I've bestowed
According to Goethe everything contains within itself every other thing
But by and by we will no longer recall this and even if we do it's not likely
The relationship between all things and all things
To find a ready place within the total significance and even disavowing it
Resonating in the dialectic of sympathy and opposition
Is hardly worth the trouble so
Coupling destruction and rebirth
If at some time and place our paths have crossed what of it
Each and every one of us and each and every thing
That we will only make the we to come
Is once more renewed and we find ourselves
All the less important we are
Growing eager again
Simply unimportant

魚罐頭

給朋友的婚禮

魚躺在蕃茄醬裡
魚可能不大愉快
海並不知道

海太深了
海岸也不知道

這個故事是猩紅色的
而且這麼通俗
所以其實是關於蕃茄醬的

Epithalamion for a Tin of Fish

Lying in its bed of tomato sauce (or is it catsup?)
Our fish may not quite relish its position;
But what does the sea know of this, in its deep abyss?
Or the shore, for that matter, no less at sea, as they say.

'Tis a tale told in scarlet (or is it cherry red?);
Whatever — a little silly this matchup;
Which is to say it is, in point of fact,
A saucy tale about catsup.

姜嫄

厥初生民
時維姜嫄
生民如何
克禋克祀
以弗無子
　　　詩經　生民

　　每逢下雨天
　我就有一種感覺
　想要交配　繁殖
　　　子嗣　遍佈
於世上　各隨各的
　　　　　方言
　　宗族
　　　　立國

　　像一頭獸
在一個隱密的洞穴
　　每逢下雨天

　　像一頭獸
　用人的方式

Jiang Yuan, Mother of the Chinese People

'Tis to the famed Jiang Yuan we trace
The earliest of our favored race;
And how this happened, let my verse
The ancient story now rehearse . . .
The Book of Poetry

Every time it rains
I get the urge
To copulate, to propagate
To spread my progeny
Across the sea, each with their own
Idiom
        Clan
Kingdom

Like a beast
In a hidden cave
Every time we have a rainy day

Like a beast
Using the human way

印刷術

沒有一個馴獸師
能令他馴養的動物
如此地聽話
史賓格勒

但是我們將如何開始我們的早餐呢
如果不先看看報紙

如何把吐司抹上奶油
把火腿煎上蛋

如果伊朗不曾攻打伊拉克
如果美滿吾妻你不逃走

The Art of Printing

> *No animal tamer*
> *ever tamed an animal*
> *as obedient as this.*
> Spengler

But how then shall we begin our breakfast
If we do not first read the paper

How will we butter our toast
Fry our ham and eggs

If Iran had not attacked Iraq
If you, my Mary Lou, did not leave me

鋸子

我想像你在我的反面行走。
在我們有限的關於宇宙的知識中
有個簡單的意義
叫做「時差」。
當我挫敗的、愉悅的
在黑夜的水域中
我們有了所謂的「構成和韻律」
像某些畫派主張的
觸及根本的原理
我貼身於黑暗中
繼續對一種鋸齒狀的真理的思考

我從事思考
鋸齒狀的
譬如一個打開的罐頭
我對於罐頭的思考如下：
罐頭的開啓依賴
一種鋸齒狀的真理

我思考，但是我睡著了
睡眠是一種古老的活動
比文明
比詩更老
我端坐苦思良久
決心不去抗拒它

The Saw

I visualize you walking on the other side from me
In our scanty understanding of the universe
We propose a simple definition
Which we call "the time difference"
Whenever I feel delicious or defeated
In the watery regions of the night
We author our "form and meter"
Like the cardinal principles
Certain schools of painting have long advanced
Enfolded by the dark
I continue my contemplation of a kind of saw-toothed-shaped truth

I engage in the contemplation
Of serration
An opened can for instance
My contemplation of the can goes thus:
The opening of a can turns
Upon a kind of saw-toothed-shaped truth

I contemplate but then I sleep
Sleep being an ancient practice
Older than civilization
Older yet than poetry
I sit and puzzle over it for hours
Resolved to not resist it

我思考睡眠
　　　當我
像一把鋸子一樣醒過來

　　我思考鋸子

I contemplate sleep
When like a saw
I drag myself awake

I contemplate the saw

Translator's Notes

The Ripest Rankest Juiciest Summer Ever

I have taken the liberty of using end-rhymes where the original has relied on subtler prosodic effects to achieve the poem's elegant fusion of languor and whimsy. The first line of the 14th couplet is rather freely translated. A more literal rendering would be: "Our guest, a student of ancient Chinese architecture, says." The phrase "the appleness of the apples" is also a translator's liberty but one which Hsia Yü incorporated into the final version of her poem.

Dreaming Beuys

For the benefit of readers unfamiliar with the work of Joseph Beuys—Beuys rhymes with Joyce, a writer with whom this late great installation artist, social visionary, and co-founder of the German Green Party and the Free International University for Creativity and Interdisciplinary Research had much in common—I have taken the liberty of adding a few proper names and phrases that do not appear in Hsia Yü's Chinese. *Pompidou* refers of course to the Musée National d'Art Moderne, Centre George Pompidou, Paris, where, in 1994, Hsia Yü saw the Beuys retrospective depicted in the poem. *Trans-Siberian Railway* is the name of the performance work or *action* (as Beuys preferred to call them) the poet describes as "an unenterable work room," a phrase borrowed from a Chinese translation of one of the numerous biographies devoted to Beuys. The quotation "The manner of the meeting was important," which does appear in the Chinese, was made in connection not with *Trans-Siberian Railway* but with a different action, *Coyote: I Like America and America Likes Me.* Performed at the Gallerie René Block in New York in 1974, this environmentalist work centered on the artist's interactions with a coyote with whom he shared a gallery space for a week. The remark in question was made to Beuys biographer Caroline Tisdall, in explanation of why, immediately upon landing at Kennedy Airport, the artist had had himself wrapped in a blanket of felt, strapped into a stretcher, and transported to the gallery in a hospital ambulance: "The manner of the meeting was important. I wanted to concentrate only on the coyote. I wanted to isolate myself, insulate myself, see nothing of America other than the coyote" (quoted in Caroline Tisdall, *Joseph Beuys We Go This Way*. London: Viollete Editions, 1998, page 170). It was, incidentally, on the flight to America for this action that Beuys draped a cloth across his face in the elephantine manner described in the poem. The term "Beckstein," which I added purely for the sound, is the brand name of the grand piano Beuys wrapped in felt for his 1966 action, *Infiltration-homogen for Grand Piano, the Greatest Twentieth-century Composer is the Thalomide Child.* Beuys's fascination with felt and fat (or lard, as I have put it) appears to have originated in an experience he had as a Luftwaffe radio operator on the Russian Front during WWII. Severely burned in a plane crash during a snowstorm over the Crimea, Beuys was rescued by a group of nomadic Tartars who kept him alive by coating him in lard and wrapping him in woolen felt. Although the story may be apocryphal, these humble materials became crucial to Beuys's art, iconography, and spiritual regeneration in the post-war era. Finally, a more literal translation of the two lines I have rendered as *For you made it state-of-the art/ World without end* would be: *Because the boredom and ennui you arrived at was boredom and ennui's/ Alpha and Omega, the beginning and the ending.* I felt the departure was necessary to prevent readers from assuming that, in alluding to "Revelations I:7," Hsia Yü was presenting Beuys as a Christ-figure when she merely meant to emphasize her thesis that Beuys brought an almost religious intensity to his installment of boredom and ennui as the new axis around which the arts would thenceforth revolve.

Continuing Our Discussion of Boredom and Ennui

The italicized phrase in French is a direct allusion to the celebrated painting by Matisse, who takes his title from the refrain of Baudelaire's "L'Invitation au voyage" ("Invitation to the Voyage"): "Là, tout n'est qu'ordre et beauté,/ Luxe, calme et volupté" ("There, where all is order, beauty,/ Luxury, calm and voluptuousness"). The two lines beginning *A city made of recollections* . . . are considerably more coherent than the corresponding lines in the original, whose meaning, as the author herself acknowledges, is anybody's guess.

Scenario for a Tango

I have expanded the title partly for the sake of the rhyme but also to flag the fact that my version of this poem is more on the order of an adaptation than a translation insofar as I have taken the liberty of casting the translation in the form of a film scenario, an idea that came to me after hearing Hsia Yü describe how much she wished she had the resources to turn this poem into a film. All the phrases typical of a film scenario, such as *Our story opens* and *Close up of the writer*, are translator's liberties. I have also taken the liberty of "beefing up" my version with a few phrases not appearing in the Chinese: *Grand Guignol* and *But then we are familiar with her modus operandi* . . . The phrase *Schmilblick avance!*, which does appear in the original, is an obscure, nonsensical coinage that briefly made its rounds on French television game shows in the 1960s. According to the poet, it is roughly equivalent to the American game show expression I have added to the following line, *And so moving on!*

Salsa

The rhyme and rhythm of my translation are much more forceful than the original. I have added a few Spanish words and phrases for flavor. *Compañera* ("female companion"), the term used by Ernesto Ché Guevara (1928-1967) to describe or address his wives, lovers, and other significant others, was added primarily for the internal rhyme. *Aye mi Cuba* ("O, my Cuba"), the title of a well-known *salsa* tune from the 1960s, when the Argentinean revolutionary left his most enduring mark on the public imagination, was added for the sake of both sound and sense. Nor does Hsia Yü quote the Spanish in her version of the line I have translated *My destiny lies in the Spanish language*, whose source is the opening to Borges's splendid poetic tribute to the German language: "*Al Idioma Alemán.*" The line "Knees that have known the long march with the outlaws of the marsh" is rather freely rendered and cobbled from two allusions to "chapters" in the romance of revolution not found in Hsia Yü's Chinese. The first is the "Long March" of 1934-35, in which the Red Army removed itself to Yenan to avoid being annihilated by Chinese Nationalist forces. The second is *Outlaws of the Marsh*, one of the inspired English titles for *Shuihuzhuan* (*The Water Margin*), the great Ming novel about rebels in Shandong much favored by writers on the left.

In the Beginning was the Written Word

Although the title plays off the familiar opening of "The Gospel According to St. John," the poem has no Christian connotations. Rather, it is concerned with the genealogy of Chinese writing, whose invention was long attributed to the mythic figure Cang Jye, who is said to have lived in the 27th century B.C.E.— hence the reference to these 5000 years.

Those Gloriously Sinful Days of Old

Porcini ("piglets") is the more familiar Italian term for what the French call *cèpes* (*Boletus edulis*), a fleshy, brown mushroom that grows among the leaf-litter of chestnut and oak trees in southern France and northern Italy, where it is highly sought for its meaty flavor.

A Personal Hell

This homage to Borges recalls several pieces by the Argentinean writer but one is reminded, in particular, of the 1940 short story "Tlön, Uqbar, Orvis Tertius," in which can be found the following passage (as translated by Alastair Reid): "For one of those gnostics, the visible universe was an illusion or, more precisely, a sophism. Mirrors and fatherhood are abominable because they multiply it and extend it."

Somehow

The French quotation means "Love does not exist but there is proof that love exists." The original is in Chinese but I liked the idea of going back to the original of the original, which was a slogan from a sort of pamper-her-with-flowers commercial Hsia Yü saw in France, where she was living when she wrote this poem.

The Mercury We So Carefully Raise

As I mentioned in my preface, the poems in the *Rub: Ineffable* collection were randomly pastiched from words and phrases culled from Hsia Yü's earlier collections. This particular poem, for example, incorporates material from at least half a dozen poems in *Ventriloquy*, several of which I have translated in *Fusion Kitsch*.

Rub: Ineffable

Skittish buffeting is a rather free extrapolation of a much simpler phrase in the Chinese: *zhuang* (literally: "jarring [it/each other]").

The Cloistered Queen and Her Invisible City

Musée des objets perdues—C'est formidable!: A museum of lost objects—that's terrific!

(A Sweet and Lingering Death)

The reference to losing the lamb has no Christian connotations. Rather, it is an allusion to the Chinese adage: *qilu wangyang* ("losing the lamb when the roads are myriad" or, as we might say in English, "adhere to the straight and narrow"). Ignoring the moral force behind such adages has been, in more ways than one, the starting point of many of Hsia Yü's most interesting departures.

L'Empire à la Fin de la Décadence

Rather than translate the title into English, I have gone back to Hsia Yü's source, the opening line of Paul Verlaine's "Langueur" ("Languor"): "Je suis l'Empire à la fin de la décadence . . ." ("I am the empire at the end of its decadence/ observing the towering white barbarians pass/ while I compose idle acrostics/ in a golden style where the languors of the sun dance . . . . A fierce ennui nauseates my soul . . ."). A fine poet and one of China's first feminists, Qiu Jin (1879?-1907) was tried and beheaded by the Manchu government after being caught sequestering arms for Sun Yat-sen's revolutionary party. There is a famous studio photograph of Qiu Jin "in drag" in most biographies of this revolutionary martyr.

Heavy Metal

The original does not use tool or toolbox metaphors but makes the genital puns through a play of Chinese pronouns and word-substitutions that cannot be reproduced in English. "Bear witness to the frailty of steel" is Michelle Yeh's inspired translation of the phrase; as it cannot possibly be bettered, I have taken the liberty of borrowing it.

And time falls like mercury

This translation and the four that follow are from a suite of fourteen sonnets. I have gone with a literal translation of the Chinese term for sonnet for fear the more familiar English term might suggest the poems in this suite bore a formal relationship to the Western sonnet, which is not the case, apart of course from sharing the same number of lines. The combined titles of the suite form a "complementary" fifteenth poem, which Hsia Yü placed at the beginning of the suite, where it serves as both a table of contents and an overture. *Spawling* is an archaic English word meaning "to spit." The original Chinese is not archaic but Hsia Yü makes occasional use of archaic words and phrases to roughen the surface of her poetry.

Leaving a sentence on the wall

Hsia Yü cannot recall the sources for the lines in quotations, although she suspects they may lie in the poetry of Paul Verlaine or Stéphane Mallarmé, whose work she was reading at the time. I have not been able to locate any lines by either of these poets which might have served as her sources. However, the phrase I have translated as *pale green as a stem* appears to echo a line from Leonard Cohen's "Sisters of Mercy": "They will bind you with love that is graceful and green as a stem." As a youth, Hsia Yü was steeped in Cohen's work and a number of her early poems reveal his influence.

Translation

Most of the poems in this last section are from Hsia Yü's first and youthful collection *Memoranda* (1983). One exception is this poem, which is a more recent and uncollected work whose style and mood set it nevertheless among Hsia Yü's earlier poetry. I have taken the liberty of using the word *veil* where the Chinese reads *rainwear*. The Chinese term (*yuyi*) is not only considerably more poetic than the English equivalent but rainwear in Taiwan tends to be made of see-through plastic. A literal translation would have reduced much of the eroticism of the closing image: *veil* seemed an appropriate substitute, especially given the tradition in the West of comparing translation to "kissing through a veil."

More and More People Wanting to Get Involved

This is another fairly recent uncollected work.

Epithalamion for a Tin of Fish

Rather than translate the epigraph, which reads "for the wedding of a friend," I thought it more interesting to incorporate the information it conveys into my version of the title. The rhyme and meter are largely my own invention. Without them the poem seemed too much like an early Richard Brautigan poem and I did not want Hsia Yü to appear derivative where she was not.

Jiang Yuan, Mother of the Chinese People

For the translation of the epigraph, I have borrowed from the splendid English of the great Victorian translator, James Legge, "earliest of our favored race."